How to Believe in God

By

Therapeutic Speaker:

Christopher Cole

This Book is for God.
I pray this book inspires you to champion into the glory God has placed upon you.
I pray this book guides you to where you need to go.

Dedicated to my Mother.

God's blessing on Earth. God's blessing to me. Beauty and life merged by love into one. My prayers were answered before I was born.

Therefore , I tell you, whatever you ask for in Prayer , Believe that you receive it, and it will be yours.
      -Mark 11:24

I wrote this for the lost. It is inspired by truth.

Table of Contents

How to Believe in God 7
God Want's You to Cultivate 13
Wisdom 16
Spirit Force 19
Obedience First 22
Believing for Forgiveness 24
Don't Rush 25
Lets get work clear 27
Enslaved 32
Giant Slayer 36
Immortality 41
Condemnation Free 48
Follow your Dharma 51
Why did Jesus Come 57
The Right Toss 58
Your Grace with God 67
No Other Way 71
Possessing the Holy Spirit 76
Get Up and Go 84
Fuel Your Fire 87
Crucial 92
Live on the Rest 96
Genesis 26:13 98
The Game of Options 106
Escaping 109
Stop Listening to Other People 110
Stop Letting Go of the Wrong Things 112
Silent on the Issues 115
Revelation Along the Way 120
Learn to Speak the Language 255
Let Go 259
Hear the Heart 269
Make Weird Noises 271
Hearing Your Calling 274
Blind Man with Three Blind Dice. 276
Samson's Death 287
Under the Law 298
Man's Discipline 302
Turning Unclean to Clean 305
To know God 309
Don't Accept It 311
True Sin 315
Heart Reviving 319
Heart Reader 323

Victory Has Been Waiting 123
Finding Direction 125
David and Goliath 127
Rappers , Super Trappers and Jesus 134
Trophy Wife 139
How the Heart Works 142
Don't be misled 147
Kingdom Living 151
Don't Run to Man 153
Let's Get to Work 156
BEING HOLY 159
Rescue Me God 160
Relationships Talk About Love 166
Doors of Destiny 176
Vision to Move Forward 179
Believe Into Victory 181

Cravings 326
Before Jesus 329
Click Over 331
Financial Savings 332
Three things I learned in India 334
What I learned from studying Confucius 337
What I learned in Chinese Martial Arts 338
Holiness with Meaning 340
A Noble Life 343

You are waiting on God and God is waiting on your spirit. 186
Fail Safe One 195
Opportunities are Bountiful 199
Bodybuilding with God 202
Provision with God 205
One thing at a time 215
What is Love 2 220
Righteous Success 225
If Only You Believe 231
Show Up So God Can Show Out 239
What Happens when You Connect with God 244
Affliction 247

IN THE BEGINNING

Why do we give thanks to Jesus ? Because he made things available for us to receive .

In the beginning God made everything available to us to subdue, and have dominion over.

Man though, allowed satan to steal the reward that came from maintaining authority. He lost his authority when he stepped out of alignment with God and did not follow through. The project was to subdue the devil, then go about creating without hinder. The blessing was to be able to see it and boldly decree it making this process achievable without toil. Anytime, you self doubt, or don't finish something -- you are allowing the effects of satan to take root , because with time he will scold you, stone you, and condemn

you for not following through.
God made us autonomous, therefore he could not force us to stay with the power he gifted us with.
The only reason why we are able to once more take hold of our dominion and power today, is because of Jesus Christ.
Through his sacrifice we were made whole.
By his blood , you have the credentials to go before

God and do Godly things within the Universe. Therefore, since satan managed to sneak in , due to Adam's self-doubt of not following through, he opened the door for satan to rob, steal and destroy all good things.

Jesus then was born and was met with a choice to sacrifice like a man but live like a God to see if God's creation was still possible of

fulfilling it's designed purpose.
With his sacrifice, Jesus restored our ability to create again.

We must stay in alignment with God and also say the simple prayer asking for Jesus to come into our hearts.
This makes it possible for us to believe in seemingly impossible and achieve it.

So say thank you Jesus and don't let satan ever win again.

How to Believe in God

1. Believe and accept what Jesus Christ has made available to you [he has to become real to you, for these gifts to become real.]
2. Undo idleness, false realities and sin.
3. Surrender to God
4. Connect with the Holy Spirit
5. Maintain the Holy Spirit
6. Create with the Holy Spirit

7. Thank god for the outcome you had with working with the Holy Spirit.
8. Inspire others to follow God and work with the Holy Spirit.

9. Once you understand that your Operating System is the Holy Spirit — things will begin to make sense. This is what a true believer in God would understand. As a believer you must understand that

once satan no longer occupies your time, you will be able to unleash your greatest potential.
Then you will grow to commit to living according to the word of God, by repeating the acts of reading , speaking , and hearing the word of God and resist ALLL temptations.
SHUT —THEM—DOWN.

DO NOT Allow bad thoughts to manifest images in your head.
Tame your tongue and learn to only speak life.
This lifestyle is essentially you accepting what God has placed inside of you.
That is dominion.
This dominion when experienced will produce a powerful force field around you everyone can see and feel.

It is your job as a believer not to go light hearted and protect with authority your territory and seek to expand it.
During this time you must realize that the power you are baring is not just for you,
but it is a tool you MUST use to shape this Earth into the Kingdom of Heaven.
Go Boldly and you shall prevail!

Give all glory and honor to God and thank Jesus Christ for the burden he bared to prepare you for this day.

God Want's You to Cultivate

So that when the time comes, you will be cultivated and capable to truly help others. Sometimes you have to send off the others—all the distractions— and enter into self refinement before one of your greatest earth defying miracles can take place. Even after Jesus just got done preforming a miracle of multiplying the fish and the bread, he later retreated to pray. There soon after , he walked on water. "Immediately Jesus made the disciples get into the boat and go on ahead of Him to the other side, while He dismissed the crowds. After He had sent them away, He went up on the mountain by Himself to pray. When evening came, He was there alone," (Matthew 14:22)

Throughout the scripture, we find instances when the Holy Spirit urges you to close the door behind you and go into focus mode. The quietness sometimes allows the spirit to flow within you. God is able to finally give you the vision of what you are suppose to do. The prayer is important, but sometimes you have to make room in your life for God to send the blessing by being quite enough to hear.

Wisdom

If wisdom is application
Then being void of wisdom means being void of accomplishment.
How can Satan keep you from accomplishment?
By occupying your heart with sin, discourse (the stuff that gets you off your course)
and undeserving unrighteousness. All of these twisted and wicked things (that which is

opposite to truthful glory) is the root cause to disbelief. The wisdom of Solomon 1:3 says that " Perverse thoughts separate men from God, and when his power is tested, it convicts the foolish; because wisdom will not enter a deceitful soul, nor dwell in a body enslaved to sin. For a Holy and disciplined spirit will flee from deceit, and will rise and depart from foolish thoughts , and will be ashamed at the approach of unrighteousness."

You will only want to run from unrighteousness if you have someplace better to run to.

That place you will be running into is the grace of God. Your mission as a believer in God is to stay in alignment with God.

Spirit Force

If you don't have discipline then you are aren't keeping truth with yourself.

If you don't have truth with yourself, you can't experience God's trust and truth,

Once you release yourself from yourself, then you can unleash your spirit upon the earth.

You were made to walk in truth, and walk in glory.

"God chose you from the beginning to be saved through sanctification by the Spirit and belief in the truth. To this he called you through our gospel, so that you may obtain the glory of our Lord Jesus Christ." 2 Thessalonians 2:13.

Once you enter this lifestyle you will run from falsehood. There will be no trap that can snare you, and you will find out that you are tapped into an unlimited source with God.

Obedience First

Obedience is what separates you from the land of nothing to the majesty of every—one of God's blessings.

Maybe you're too busy praying.

Maybe you're too busy doing what you're not suppose to.

Maybe you're too busy figuring out how not to be generous with others.

Maybe you're listening to the wrong people. Any of these pre-occupations keeps you out of the receptive alignment you need to be in to receive from God.

Believing for Forgiveness

Matthew 6:14 explains "For if you forgive others their trespasses [their reckless and willful sins], your heavenly Father will also forgive you."

If you believe others can be forgiven, then you know you can be forgiven.

End of discussion.

God has forgiven you.

Now go and accept it.

Don't Rush

The longer the step the easier the climb.
Don't be fooled.
Rushing is just a twisted version of getting some place ahead of time.
When in actuality you can do it like God and call things into existence.
Stop being afraid to do it like God,
because you were made to do it like God.
Time bends to your bow.

Your words shape destiny. And your actions reinforce it.

Believe in God and you will be able to have enough belief to create the Universe.

Lets get work clear

God gives you the power to create wealth without stress or toil.

But domination does not rest with the person who is lazy.

Why?

Because a lazy idle person is so clouded with nothing that they would fail to use, or see the blessing if it came tapping on their shoulder — thus wasting it.

Why?

Because they lay there in condemnation, self paralyzing and rejecting God's dreams.
With this being said.
There is no contradiction with working hard and still being at rest.
A person at rest, is a person who is creating with divine power.
Have you ever talked to a lazy idle person who feel's that they have missed out

on their dreams and opportunity?
There is no rest to be found within them.
Just a sate of passionately running in a circle.
God does not want this for us, because we were designed to be busy creating new things.
Therefore when the scripture in 2 Thessalonians 3:6 warns us not to be idle it is explaining to the people, that the example we found

in God was a person who was working hard and toiling to get it right, for the sake of creating something better for us to have.

Now that Jesus figured out and blessed us with it.

We get the best of both worlds.

We must actively be focused on working to establish a foundation in our life. But in duel we also inherit the grace and the Kingdom.

This opens doors for us through favor, and gives us the ability to righteously dominate and to gain wealth without stress or toil, as it explains in Deuteronomy 8:18 But this is the life you must believe for and expect. This life is only made possible by believing in and through Jesus Christ, by what he helped make available for us.

Enslaved

Many people are dating and married to enslaved people.
In order to run free into new territory God has made available for the family, one has to leave bondage behind.
Whether it's the lack of self-esteem or actual bondage, a man , a woman , must vehemently take control

over their territory with casting the devil out of it. You can't receive the spirit of GOD , if you are maintaining the spirit of fear and slavery. Romans 8:15 says "For you did not receive a spirit of slavery that returns you to fear, but you received the Spirit of sonship, by whom we cry, "Abba!
Father!" The Spirit Himself t estifies
with our spirit that we are God's children. And if we

are children, then we are heirs: heirs of God and co-heirs with Christ—if indeed we suffer with Him, so that we may also be glorified with Him"

This means that the internal voice you hear , should be the voice of God not the voice of fear.

If you hear any other voice besides God's - cancel it. Proclaim immediately " God did not give me the spirit of bondage, slavery, or fear, but one of a sound mind, in direct communication with him discerning all righteous things."

Sometimes people have to get out of the relationship with themselves before they can enter the relationship with God, and this absolutely has to happen before they can fully be in a relationship with someone else.

Giant Slayer

People will convince you that you are inadequate, but all you need to do is continue in your rest, towards victory anyway. They said to David " you are not able to go against this philistine to fight with him; for you're but a youth ....
1 Samuel 17:33
Well we now know David went on to defeat Goliath anyway .

A lot of people are paralyzed with fear so much that they cannot move forward.
Out of fear they think why even start ---
I'm so late anyway….
All I do is sit around and waste time --- so I'm not going to start , because I should of started earlier.
I'm condemned because when God told me to move I waited.
No !

Your blessing is waiting on you to use it.
It starts when you start,
It stops when you stop.
God is like a smart faucet, it doesn't run unless you are standing in front of it, making use of the blessing.
The scripture shows us that the divine oil stoped running-- when the widow had no more pots in place to fill.
So it's easy to be defeated and not even start by

walking with the false fear of satan that if you start now , if you go now , you're only gonna meet defeat and be hurt because you started to late with hesitation .
Don't be swindled , get up , and move forward onto victory.

--- when you enter into the rest , this fear will become null and void anyway , because you have began to operate in the rest and the boldness takes over. The boldness strikes down anything contrary to the vision at hand God gave you.

Just like David, you continue into the battle anyway to defeat your giant.

Immortality

Immorality separates you from your immortality.
Ever feel weak and lost after you sin?
I believe that believing in God is a matter of preserving yourself from falling into that trap.
In order to do this , you must believe in God by using your strength in preserving things like your sexual energy until you meet your wife.

Why?
Because God knew the powerful forces which stood to keep man and woman from their divine destiny.

"But because of the temptation to sexual immorality, each man should have his own wife and each woman her own husband." 1 Corinthians 7:2

It's not that God designed a boring system called life. He on the contrary wants you to fully be able to

maximize out of life every good thing it has to offer.
If satan can cause you to fall to the door of condemnation through things like sex, he can trip you up.
God knows the immortal power you hold, and he wants us to be able to walk in it.
But you cannot walk in it if you feel condemned.
And for most, condemnation comes

heavily from being sexually immoral.

However, God wants us to enjoy sex.

Therefore, sex within a marriage is critical and in fact should be used as a tool to beat satan at his own game.

Why trade perversion that leaves you broke and desperate for fiery love that leaves you regenerated , happy , and bold?

Therefore, you will live void of grief and condemnation and be able to use your power to achieve many good things on Earth by subduing temptation.

Why let any temptation or immoral act stand in the way of this?

If you believe in God, you will treat yourself like a temple of the Holy Spirit. In fact God cares more for us to treat ourselves like temples then to build a temple for him.

1 Corinthians 6:18 "Flee from sexual immorality. Every other sin a person commits is outside the body, but the sexually immoral person sins against his own body. Or do you not know that your body is a temple of the Holy Spirit within you, whom you have from God? You are not your own, for you were bought with a

price. So glorify God in your body."
Why?
Because the Holy Spirit dwells within us.

Condemnation Free

Condemnation outweighs hard work. And passion outweighs death.
That's why God's answer isn't sweat and toil , but to live condemnation free. If you live condemnation free you'll allow God to go to work delivering passion. Paralyzation comes from condemnation. The reason why people stay in their dark cloud is because they are

condemned with the reality that they have already wasted enough time so they are convinced that they are late and have missed all of their opportunities.

With believing in God, you will want to grow into a life not placed around fear, because fear destroys faith. And with no faith , there is no certainty.

If you cannot do it out of certainty do not do it out of fear.

God has provided us with our beloved sleep.
So if you can't enter the rest, it's only because you are allowing something to stop you.
Until you begin to resist the devil, you won't see the breakthrough that moves you to a higher place.
Your aggression with breaking through to your future, is a direct result of this breakthrough into becoming bold.

Follow your Dharma

Dharma is doing that which you know you are meant to be doing at that particular moment.

If you walk with God , talk with God
the Holy Spirit will come over you and you will know in your heart what to do and when to do it.

Sometimes you are called to give to one person, and pass up the next— not out of pride, but out of discernment.

You are designed to make moves when God says to make moves.

" Consider this: Whoever sows sparingly will also reap sparingly, and whoever sows generously will also reap generously. Each one should give what he has decided in his heart to give, not out of regret or compulsion. "
2 Corinthians 9:6

The ability to live with discernment is a gift of the Holy Spirit.

Allowing you to skip the trap of feeling regret. Regret designed to keep you from sowing good things in the future.

The spirit wanted Jesus to inspire breakthrough when others wanted to sit around and fear. When Jesus multiplied the fish, he asked for seemingly useless ingredients. But what we learned is that Jesus was asking by his discernment of the spirit - exactly what was required. These spiritual moves made available the miracle to take place out of faith.

Sometimes believing in God is listening to what God is instructing you to do, over what man say's needs to be done— even if the men say these are the rules of God.

Again we see this illustrated by Jesus when he was within the synagogue.

"Once again Jesus entered the synagogue, and a man with a withered hand was there. In order to accuse Him, they were watching to see if He would heal on the Sabbath.

Then Jesus said to the man with the withered hand, "Stand up among us." And He asked them, "Which is lawful on the Sabbath: to do good or to do evil, to save life or to destroy it?"

But they were silent.

Jesus looked around at them with anger and sorrow at their hardness of heart. Then He said to the man, "Stretch out your hand." So he stretched it out, and it was restored. (Mark 3:1)

Jesus wanted us to know that God is not defined by man, and is capable to move through and by the

Holy Spirit at all and any times.
So when the spirit urges, even if the world does not see it as commonsense , you have to make the moves.

Why did Jesus Come
Jesus came to vouch to God that his creation was in fact capable of fulfilling it's purpose.

The Right Toss

If the flesh can spot a lie.
The spirit can spot a fake.
It's imperative you grow
enough to understand the
difference between wasting
your blessing, and
cultivating it.
If you listen to the world,
you might be apt to believe
that a person who believes
in God and has seed to sow
has to give all of themselves

at all times; even give their last, be broke and a joke.
NOPE!
Thats not in the word of God!
Sorry.
Try again.
In this scenario the concept of sacrifice is twisted.
What good is sprouting seed tossed into the sewer? Versus seed that knows it's value and waits for the perfect plot of land to plant itself into.

Plant your seed where God directs you to. Don't waste it where the world compelled you to.
2 Corinthians 9:8 says "...Each one should give what he has decided in his heart to give, not out of regret or compulsion. For God loves a cheerful giver." If you believe in God, you will know where and when. With God you will grow enough to not only plant your seed, you will be able

to watch it grow, weed out the specific problems which threaten it's growth and be able to harvest it.
When this happens you won't need to listen to what others say ,
or even care what it looks like to other people.
You'll have the bold discerning faith to know what is to come and that the devil has already been defeated.

You will feel safe to toss your seed where God instructs you to , without hesitation or limitation.

Be cautious for the one who wants you to reveal your weaknesses. Beware of the person who inspires you to fall upon your weakness. God did not make you weak. And if the flesh is weak the spirit can be strong.

Sometimes to resist the temptation , you have to

resist certain people. Shut them down! Keep it moving. A lion does not let random animals come play in their territory.

We can take a lesson from Samson and Deli'lah, after several attempts to defeat Samson, she asked him for his secrets to his strength. Even after proving she sought only his destruction she still possessed the ability to say "How can you say , 'I love you,' when your

heart is not with me? You have mocked me these three times and not told me wherein your great strength lies." (Judges 16:15)
Though, the wows may come, you must avidly reject them.

Hold steadfast to not wasting your time with satan, or sharing your secrets with the adversary. Sometimes you have to ignore even the closes to you in order to connect with what God is directing you in. If you can learn to do this then you earn the right to be able to help people in an influential way. Jesus had to ignore his disciples in the sacrifice that he would end up in actuality, helping them as a group in a much greater way than they ever would've expected. He had to leave his disciples alone and care for himself only in his purpose which was to leave, go into fasting to become that which he had to become to actually be able to help in a meaningful way.

Your Grace with God

When you step out of your grace you had with God by Christ Jesus , you experience condemnation. You do not receive condemnation from God. "Therefore there is now no condemnation for those who are in Christ Jesus. For in Christ Jesus the law of the Spirit of life has set you free from the law of sin and death...." The only time you fall into condemnation according to the scripture is when you fail to believe in and to reject God. When fail to forgive yourself. If you can't forgive yourself , you can't accept God's forgiveness. The only condemnation comes from you, urging you to enter back into the perceived bondage of the world. Every time the bible says " And the sons of Israel again did what was evil in the sight of the lord……." they fell into the hands of the enemy. This land of death and bondage is one Jesus came to give us the power to avoid. Therefore, Jesus restored back to us our Godly dominion.

Without it, every time we make mistakes we would enter into bondage.

Them days are over. Therefore, if you are living in bondage, it is due to your own doing. Let it go.

No Other Way

You must seek God , resist the devil and he has to flee from <u>you</u>.

- James 4:7

I start here because until you clean out the fridge you can't put new wholesome food into it.
If God blesses us with the fruits of the spirit then we need a clean place to put it so that it can go to work for

us — so that it can help multiply good things in our life.

"And no one pours new wine into old wineskins. Otherwise, the wine will burst the skins, and both the wine and the wineskins will be ruined. No, they pour new wine into new wineskins." - Mark 2:22

This says the word of God. I use it as an example to illustrate the necessity cleaning. Jesus already made you clean, but sometimes you have to be the one who feels clean, to allow any good blessings to flow. If you feel dirty, you feel condemned. And if you feel condemned, you will be in a state of spiritual standing not to let your blessings flow.

2 Timothy 2:21 says "So if anyone cleanses himself of what is unfit, he will be a vessel for honor: sanctified, useful to the

Master, and prepared for every good work."

God already possess the good work for you, it is just time for you to step up to the plate to receive it. Understanding this will allow you to have more confidence to enter into the rest of knowing things have to work out for you— and you have the power to bring the Kingdom of Heaven to Earth by faith. It is waiting for you to get a grip over all your weaknesses that cause you to stop, and to accept the righteousness God gave you.

Possessing the Holy Spirit

The divine Holy Spirit needs a place where there is obedience and willingness to follow through. Gradually, you were designed to become a master over time so that you won't run out of time while on your mission. You are meant to be preforming greater miracles then Jesus Christ did, all while being alive here on Earth.

Bring your divine Holy Spirit alive on Earth so that it can begin delivering you your blessings from Heaven requires your partnership. Plant good seed, cultivate it and do not forget to harvest it.

Believing in God is essentially accepting that everything is on pause until you hit play, the beautiful movie of your destiny has already been created, and now it is time for other people to be able to watch it.

Get started now!

And pull things from the realm of impossibility into the land of possibility by working with God and all the tools he has given you. In Mark 10:27 Jesus said " With man these things are impossible, but with God all things are possible." Listen to Jesus, he has already spoken it into reality that if you work with God , by believing in his power and connecting your effectiveness through him, you will be able to do the impossible.

All your dreams, desires and fulfillment's are awaiting you to bring them down from Heaven.

You have to have the faith to believe— the God type of faith that is meant to shift and create things.

Help God make sense, by unleashing your greatness

through the power he has given you and give him praise for it!

The time is far from over for talkers to run free, now it is decision making time to resist the devil, submerge yourself in the word of God, listen to your heart , equip yourself with a God type of attitude and start producing fruit bearing results; that is belief in God.

The good so called "holy person" who only stands still

does not show their belief in God as much as the person who goes to work in the Holy Spirit, meaning they are about God's business producing "greater works than these." (John 14:12 : Jesus said whoever believes in me will do these same works I have done…and even greater works than these).

Prove you are connected to a higher power by proving to yourself that you can get it started and get it done. How would a new power plant hold up to an old one, if the new one didn't even produce enough energy to keep it's own light's on, let alone provide enough energy for a whole block? People who are strongly connected to God become strong from practicing, walking and living in the spirit. You must face temptation, fear and depression , and command it off your territory. Your knees may be gettin' weak at the preachers door, but be reminded God has delivered you from all forms of death. So although you may enter into dark places, and do dark things, you can bring yourself back into the light.

You stay in your darkness for however long you choose to keep the lights off.

Get Up and Go

Get Up and Go, when God says So
get up , get going ,
tie your shoes get going
stop dreaming and get going.
Judges 7:15 says " Get up get going…." This is what Gideon did towards going to win the victory.
He moved when God told him to move, and did the things God told him to do in preparation, and when the

time came to get up ,
go ,and conquer, he did it!
We must receive the blessing God gave us, that is the Holy Spirit.
The Holy Spirit is the source through which we get directions on how to prepare to overcome the obstacles and goals we want to over come.
It is only up to us to be receptive and appreciative enough to hear the directions and follow them.

God only operates at the right time. So when he says to get up and get going, your moment is then. Take advantage of it.

Fuel Your Fire

Sow generously into preparing for your calling and you shall reap generously the harvest. 2 Corinthians 9:6 says "Consider this: Whoever sows sparingly will also reap sparingly, and whoever sows generously will also reap generously."

Those who sow generously reap generously , but before we arrived to this point in the scripture it was just being explained a few verses earlier, that a person with a gift , needs to be in the proper state to receive harvest from it. Meaning they need to have been preparing mentally for it.

No matter how talented, or blessed you may be, satan is waiting to play off of your lack of belief in yourself and in God.

You have to acknowledge that even briefly before you

have it physically, you have to live with the blessing now; that is visualize it in your mind, and feel it in your heart — you only receive what you are tuned in to receive.

This is the value of being in accordance with God. Believing in God is not merely talking about the belief or what is to come , but it includes working on it vibrantly , proving that it is on its way.

So you must be generous with yourself when it comes to living cheerfully in expectancy.

Cheerful enough to radiate huge amounts of positive energy towards the thing and lifestyle you are expecting.

Think of it as adding fuel to the fire.

You may have the Godly fire inside of you but it is up to you to add fuel to it.

The fuel is every positive thing you shout, and negative thing you reject. If you want to have great wealth to share with others, then you should never find yourself in a moment of accepting states of doubt about being in debt.
Don't fuel that fire with your energy.
Sow generously into the fire of your expectant future—which is totally debt free!

Crucial

It is crucial to distinguish the vast importance of what Jesus has done for the rest of the world who were not within "Nahala" a defined circle; meaning all those who were not in one particular tribe within one particular region or inheritance. There was a time when there was a boundary that could stand between you and God. Now, however, Jesus has taken away that boundary if you only believe.

Jesus today, calls those who believe in him to receive the inheritance he has guaranteed for us.

Which is being placed in the righteousness of God to in fact enter into the Kingdom of God and be a disciple within it.

As it says in 1 Samuel 3:1 "And the word of the lord was rare in those days; there was no frequent vision."

Meaning God is able to communicate with people through discerning visions, but only certain people back then got that blessing. Whether it was the law , religion, lineage, or tradition the world was able to segregate God.
Through Jesus' sacrifices, he shifted God from just dwelling with the select few, to an open boundary to select you.

Now that you are selected, what are you doing with your power?
Are you just dreaming, or bringing your vision to reality?

Live on the Rest

Debt cannot face you , if faith is with you.

The widow and her pot of oil found in 2 Kings 4: 1-7 exposed to us the power of an obedient miracle.

" with debt facing her.... he said... sell your oil, and pay your debt, and your sons can live on the rest."

Ask God for the supernatural multiplying miracle. Then shut the door behind you and get to work.

Get your wealth , pay your debts and live on the rest! Amen.

Genesis 26:13

" The man got richer and richer by the day until he was very wealthy."
I want to get richer and richer by the day.
How did he get richer and richer by the day?
He decreed things, stood his position, and spoke the future into being— he used the blessing , and the inheritance God gave him :
" Issac named the well Esek

(Quarrel)… he named the next one Sitnah (Accusation) …. he went on and made yet another well, he name it Reho'both (Wide Open Spaces) , saying 'Now God has given us plenty of space to spread"

Issac could of been content with the first two well's but he expected perfection from God promises and that kept him going until he established the perfect well, the one which was with wide open space , following with abundant provision. When that well had came about , he founded it, named it and went onto the next land— that means he recognized God's blessing when he saw it and kept it moving.

The blessing made Issac richer and richer , he did not have to make himself richer and richer, all he had to do is keep operating in the blessing.

His father Abraham was blessed and loved by God. Therefore, this inheritance is what made Issac blessed by God. You too have an inheritance from Jesus Christ. Know that God has given you more than a little blessing, but the whole unlimited expanse of Heaven's blessings.
So although you may know God has ordained tremendous wealth for you, it is up to you to keep

moving, keep founding new things for people to gain something from. If you have a mission greater than yourself, you will be walking in God's purpose for your life, because you are ordained to give the world your special gift.

Next,

Don't be idle with the blessing God gave you. Do something with it and God will do something great with you.

Also expect, that you get blessed abundantly by God even when others don't, simply by you believing in God and being his child. In the scripture of Genesis 26, God said " I will bless you, I will give to you and your decedents all of these lands… because Abraham obeyed my voice…."
God is telling us, today, that because of Jesus, we inherit God's entire Kingdom.

That means we can be anywhere in the world , and if we only believe in our hearts his promise we too shall inherit. Issac was among the Philis'tines, people who did not believe like Issac's people believed —so guess what—they were not blessed as Issac was blessed " the man became rich…. so that the Philis'tines had envied him."
It matters if you believe.

And it's not even God's fault if you aren't blessed, because, God isn't selecting blessing based off what you can do, blessing is based off if you can accept it or not. So the game to be won, is up to you to win. This is the power of Jesus. So thank you Jesus for what he has done for you!

The Game of Options

Satan loves to give you a bunch of options ; In the hopes it can blind you from taking the only option that is meant for you.

Stop revealing your plan so loudly. If Issac had not told Esau what his plan was, his mother would not have heard it and told Jacob how to prepare for deception.

If you want to beat Satan at his own game, don't even talk much about it.

See it as quietly as God gave it to you and set about with quick boldness to complete it. Let your praise to God be the loudest thing heard.

Too often , we repeat the plan, ask others for counsel on the plan and do everything but accomplish the plan.

Imagine if Peter loudly asked the guards to confirm what the angel had just told him to do to escape!?! He would not of had a chance for escape!

Escaping

Sometimes you have to become imprisoned to have a place to escape from. Your imperfection has always been your opportunity for perfection.

Stop Listening to Other People

A man who has the blessing of God, but listens to other people on what to do with it, is cursed.

Issac had the power of God's blessing but kept getting swindled by his wife, because she kept telling him what to do with it— either directly, or indirectly.

Just as Adam listened to Eve, he was told from God ahead of time what to do, but still fell into disobedience by the direction of someone-else. Women and men who are obedient to God, reap the harvest God quietly ordains for them. If God told you what to do , then your plan should be to leave all of other people's concerns alone and be about your Father's business.

And close the door behind you.

Stop Letting Go of the Wrong Things

God has shown me that Christians like to let go of everything but strong holds. They let go of responsibility, commitments, hard work, discipline, generosity, love, patience; but expect God to come through, to fill in the voids.
They think that these other "pre-occupations" holds

them up from the presence of the lord. When in actuality the only thing holding them back, is in fact the one thing they refuse to let go of. That is the strong hold.

Release that, and all the other things will strengthen. You will gain a clear mind of discernment to know what to delegate time to, and where to maneuver.

You'll at that moment except the present Jesus left for you.
That is a life, and life more abundantly.

Silent on the Issues

You can only walk by faith and not by sight if you have grown enough to know from God where it is, you are going.

Early in my growth cycle I used to be afraid, thinking faith had to be blind. When really the only blindness, is that which comes from Satan. With God , you are given clarity.

As the scripture states , the wicked (twisted) are like a "troubled sea" (Isaiah 57:20) That is because they desperately do not know where to go in life— they have no passion to use their faith on. God does not work that way. If you are experiencing blindness and a lack of clarity, perhaps, you are being swindled by evil forces "Jesus rebuked the impure spirit….'You deaf and mute spirit..he said…I command you to come out!" Later the scripture goes on to reveal that the spirit Jesus casted out came out only by fasting. Sometimes , you have to let go of the flesh to enter into a spiritual rest of gaining supernatural knowledge to know what to do. If you can't hear the Holy Spirit and cannot see the visions God has for you, you need to take a moment to command this clarity into your life. And fast from the worlds visions.

Then once you can see clearly where it is you are going in life, you can use your power of faith, and begin to walk into it.

You walk by faith by walking towards your vision, even if that vision is invisible to other people. Satan's real-estate is blindness. God's real-estate is sight. Blindness is located right next to time. If you allow

Satan to maintain his real-estate in your life , he can make sure that you are late towards your destiny, and he makes sure to add poverty and sorrow with it.

If you are standing upon clarity , and grant God his real-estate in your life , he will grant you the sight to move past time, commanding things into existence, and adds wealth and no sorrow with it.

Revelation Along the Way

God prefers the man who works to the man who prays and attributes no work behind it. What are you doing with the talents God has given you?

Because what the world might consider a sinner, God considers forgiven, and if
this person has belief in God and commits work to the vision, then surely he is the

bold disciple who is using the faith God gave him. "What is the benefit, my fellow believers, if someone claims to have faith but has no [good] works [as evidence]? Can that [kind of] faith save him? [No, a mere claim of faith is not sufficient—genuine faith produces good works.]" (James 2:14 AMP)

Be encouraged, your condemnation needs to be washed away, because there

is no death Jesus has left untouched which can hold you back in life.
Stop quarreling and leaving yourself behind.
Get up and live righteously. You are good enough to be bold, to have passion and to use it.

Victory Has Been Waiting

No evil strategies can overcome you — when you believe in God.
Because no evil strategies can defeat God. And Romans 8:15 shows that you were given God's winning Spirit when he adopted you.
You are his creation.
A creation which is designed to be a creator.
You have so much power to create, that when you realize

the reward, you can't help but give thanks to God! "For you have not received a spirit of slavery leading again to fear [of God's judgment], but you have received the Spirit of adoption as sons [the Spirit producing sonship] by which we [joyfully] cry, "Abba! Father!" (Romans 8:15)
Therefore, victory is waiting on you to get it right.
Use your Godly sight to make it right.

Finding Direction

God's direction can be compared to following your first mind. But let's be clear, God communicates through your heart.

It's up to you to make your mind up to go along with it or not.

   If it doesn't go through the heart before the mind, it is not divine.

God works through the spirit which is inside of you to

produce the miracles that are in your head. It's just a thought until your action turns it into a reality.

Your heart is the throttle to faith producing destiny. That is why a cold heart towards God can't do much of anything but allow Hell to take over their life.

David and Goliath

David accepted the challenge,
spoke the victory and addressed the reality as it would be.
Just as David, you are perfectly fitted to bring victory into your life and destroy the giants that creep.
David also knew that he needed the ball in his court, even if it seemed like he

would be at a greater disadvantage.

"Then Saul dressed David in his garments and put a bronze helmet on his head, and put a coat of mail (armor) on him. Then David fastened his sword over his armor and tried to walk, [but he could not,] because he was not used to them. And David said to Saul, "I cannot go with these, because I am not used to them.""

In order to achieve the impossible, sometimes you have to take or make a path that does not make sense to the current status quo. But in order for you to be victorious you have to stand in assurance to what your heart and the Holy Spirit is instructing you to do is correct.

Take that path. The one you feel is the right one for you, the one where you can still see yourself achieving victory. It may seem impossible , but like I said God thrives on the impossible.

"Then David said to the Philistine, 'You come to me with a sword, a spear, and a javelin, but I come to you in the name of the Lord of hosts"

Stand boldly and know who you wit.

If you with God, if you send forward the Lord of Hosts,

nothing but victory can be got.
Enter into battle with speaking the outcome.
" This day the Lord will hand you over to me, and I will strike you down and cut off your head." (1 Samuel 17:46)

The battle is the lords— it has been won by God, and he handed it over to you— the victory, because he loves you "for the battle is the

Lord's and He will hand you over to us."(1 Sam. 17:46) Defeat the enemy with his own tactics. 1 Samuel 17:51 says that David "grasped his sword (Goliath) and drew it out of its sheath and killed him, and cut off his head with it."

Also,

when you win , don't forget where you came from. Saul asked him, "Whose son are you, young man?" And David answered, "*I am* the son of your servant Jesse of Bethlehem." (1 Samuel 17:58)

Never feel disadvantaged because of your background.

Little did Saul know, this is the background God was using to inspire the royal lineage for bringing the Lord and Savior Jesus Christ into the world.

Rappers, Super Trappers and Jesus

why does the world phene for rappers and super trappers?

Because those are the people who are boldly moving in a particular direction.

a super trapper
has extreme discipline and a small refined circle.

they are focused on taking over new territory and defending the one's they have.
they subdue their enemies and subdue their land.
you don't get it twisted with them.
You get it right.
Family means a lot
Honor and truth does too.
They don't whisper when they talk , they scream and they shout.

they know there may be a lot of women , but there's only one woman they can trust

they could careless about what other people think.

because they have vision and they gonna make it happen.

they delegate and terminate branches that are not producing fruit.

They don't run and beg, they find a way to make it happen.

the only downfall is the lack of beloved sleep at night , and if their foundation is built upon unrighteousness then they fall.

Where is this boldness at in the church????

Jesus came to show us, that we could live as boldly as a supper trapper, but with the heart of God.
If we combined the boldness with the

righteousness God has blessed us with , we would not fail.

We would not fall.

If we worked for good wholesome things and cultivated , subdued and cleaned wholesome territory — boldly— then we would establish the Kingdom of Heaven on Earth for people to enjoy.

Trophy Wife

If he cannot focus on just one woman that is because he did not focus on God before you.

If your man is busy talking to you that's because he it's not busy talking with God.

If you want to love her. Love her like God would.

Fight her battles for her and just hand her the victories.

Fight the battles for the family without complaint,

and hand her the Gold CUP , the trophy .
That's a trophy wife.
A woman who when you win, can be handed your divinely earned blessings in life also known as trophies, which she then will be able to appreciate. A strong trophy wife knows how to carry and cultivate them and not squander the blessings for the family. She will know to plant it as

foundational seed for the entire family.

In order for your wife to have something to plant. You have to be a Man and receive the seeds of victory God has ordained for you.

How the Heart Works

Your heart doesn't work with time,
    it discerns then earns.
The mind however, sets out about reasoning with time on how a thing can get accomplished.
This is why Jesus says not to labor or try to store up possessions
instead Jesus calls you to dwell with the Kingdom.

Those who dwell within the kingdom dwell with the Holy Spirit.

And the Holy spirit is the channel through which God can deliver your blessings from heaven , which never ruin.

Therefore, if your heart walks with your spirit then it is your spirits responsibility to discern where to turn. This takes you out of the burden of laboring a path.

Labor as a definition means to perform labor; exert one's powers of body or mind; work; toil.

If you follow your heart, you won't have to waste time in your mind trying to figure out what to do. You will just see what to do and do it.

Luke 12 —

"Consider how the wild flowers grow. They do not labor or spin.

'Do not be afraid, little flock, for your Father has been

pleased to give you the kingdom....For where your treasure is, there your heart will be also.

Your heart knows where the party is at. It's mission is to get your body there.

If you feed it corruptible things, it will recede.

But if you feed your heart the word of God, it will exceed your greatest expectations.

Nothing will be able to stop you.

Certainty will be your coat rack.

Don't be misled

Don't misunderstand what Jesus says.
God wants you to have wealth, he just doesn't want you to have to beg man for it. Or selfishly try to store it up for yourself.
Luke 12:13 says
"….Someone in the crowd said to him (Jesus), 'Teacher, tell my brother to divide the inheritance with me."

Jesus went on to explain that your life is not made up of man's riches.
If you have God's riches, you will always be richer.
You won't eat in vain,
and you won't dwell in pain.
You are designed to inherit the Kingdom of Heaven.
One which leaves you operational.
Instead of storing up for yourself, you will have wealth stored up for you.

Releasing your mind from the toil of figuring it out, making room for your heart to be able to influence your mind to give freely, where things need to be given.
You won't fear going broke. You will simply be able to give generously.
While still in return being blessed abundantly.
Being rich just means you have a whole bunch of fruit that is sitting there waiting to spoil. However operating

in the blessing of God is just like being a branch that is capable of producing new fruit season after season and it never spoils.

"He that trusteth in his riches shall fall: but the righteous shall flourish as a branch." - Proverbs 11:28

So tell me , who's really rich? At least one of the two don't have to worry about paying to keep the freezer on.

Kingdom Living

How will we know if we are operating within the Kingdom of God ?
We will know by the results we produce.
Matthew 12:28 reveals the message of Jesus, and how he preformed miracles.
Miracles which we have the ability to do as well.
"But if it is by the Spirit of God that I drive out demons, then the kingdom

of God has come upon you."

God wants us to exhibit the culture of heaven — on earth.

Many rich scholars of today say that if you mirror the habits and actions of the successful you will be successful. Well apply that philosophy to Jesus, and you will be able to live also as he did.

Don't Run to Man

Don't run to man, when God is the one calling you. Too often, we get inspiration from God to do something, only to let that vision go, due to the response we seek from other people.

1 Samuel 3:4 shows this principle loudly. " Then the lord called, 'Samuel! Samuel! ' and he said, " Here I am!" and ran to Eli and said 'Here I am, for you called me.' But he said, 'I

did not call; lie down again.' So he went and lay down. And the lord called again, 'Samuel!' And Samuel arose and went to Eli, and said ' Here I am, for you called me.' But he said, ' I did not call, my son ; lie down again.".. " if he calls you, you shall say , " Speak, Lord for your servant hears."

If you want to believe in God.

You're gonna have to say Speak Lord! And stop

listening to others to going to lay down.

To believe in God , you have to begin to take hold of your power, and offer your obedience to God.

Move on it!

Let's Get to Work.

If work ethic is weak it is because you have nothing meaningful to work for. Demand your purpose be revealed to you and over time you will demand it become acknowledge by the world.

It can only happen after you accept your life lessons and repent your weaknesses. If you leave your weaknesses in the bucket by Jesus , he can carry them away from you.

Your bucket has your name on it and it has been by his cross waiting to send your garbage to hell, to allow you to reveal Heaven. Choose life over death.

Death is being void of Godly revelation, unable to fully live in your power yielding dominion— being able to birth your righteous destiny. Don't let satan set your life up to fall like domino's , uproot sinful discourse that serves to push you off course.

Demand a solid foundation for your life, and don't forget to maintain it for your family.

Demand you have wealth to share with those you want to share it with.

God wants you to win the silent auction of life.

BEING HOLY

Being Holy is not a matter of doing things for someone else, it is a matter of doing better things for yourself.

Rescue Me God

God can send Angels to rescue you. But you have to be ready to be rescued. As Peter was being rescued an Angel came to him and said " Get up quickly" not <u>slowly</u>. Sometimes to take advantage of the divine moment of opportunity requires a quick moving mind and receptive heart. The blessing is that if you are calm enough to hear God, the spirit of God will come and instruct you in what to do, how to make moves at particular times. If you are obedient, you are then taking your inheritance of grace.

Acts 12:8 said "Suddenly an angel of the Lord appeared and a light shone in the cell. He tapped Peter on the side and woke him up, saying, "Get up quickly." And the chains fell off his wrists. 8 'Get dressed and put on your sandals' said the angel.

Peter did so, and the angel told him, "Wrap your cloak around you and follow me." Jesus came to give us a chance to live like this once again. If you believe in God through Christ Jesus , then you can accept the gift God gave you, which is the ability to work directly with heaven in establishing a good life here on earth.

If you stand upon the word of God which is found in the bible, then you can command chains broken off of you, and they have to break.

Jesus is the reason why you have this power today. NOBODY ELSE, not even God. God was and is the LOVE cause for this — the author of it. But don't be like King Herod. Give credit and thanks for what was given to you.

When they ask who did it? Say : God did it!

Give God praise, for it is good to give God praise. The person who appreciates the gift giver for the gift, shall surely be more likely to use the gift given.

If you believe in God, then you can believe that you have the power of God dwelling within you- and use the gift. Get up and run. You are starting to use the gift by believing in God that way.

Do not let your power go to waste.

Believing in God is not playing religion , it is living abundantly and boldly as a lion.

Relationships Talk About Love

What is love?

Love my friends is anticipation.
Jesus loved us, so he anticipated our needs before we even knew we had them, and he solved a problem before we even came on the scene, because he had us in mind.

He knew our weakness and blindness to the Holy Spirit. So he preformed miracles using the Holy Spirit to teach us how to do the same. He exhibited the power of faith to calm storms, and questioned why do we not do the same? The power he had , he invested in us as an inheritance for us to use in establishing Heaven on Earth.

So with Jesus' love to us, he set us up good. The Kingdom of Heaven is at hand, but it is waiting for your hands to go to work in establishing it.

Now that we know love is anticipation, then we know if a man loves a woman, he anticipates her needs and meets them.

A good man is able to care to understand her, for the purpose of fulfilling where she has lack.

For example.

If she cooks for you all the time, don't just say thank you. Surprise her with kitchen craft she once did not have — and the kitchen she once always dreamed about!

Deliver to her thousand dollar gift cards to the top grocery stores, to give her pride for what she does. Because if she is a good woman, she will love what she does for you, because she loves you.

You love her by anticipating she might need some help loving you.

The best man though, is the one that can take care of problems for her—that she didn't even know she had, then leave the room.

….Jesus took care of our problems and went back to Heaven.

You don't even have to be there to flash what you did for her.
Romantically——— let her find out.
She then will begin to see , WOW 'he does love me. Because he cares about the things which effect me.'

I hear all the time that women are audible , meaning they respond to talk and sound.

Well let me set the record straight.

Women need action.
Men need talk.

   Remember Eve's talk , got Adam into action.

I believe that women have the power to say words to a man that can make him think he is Hercules, and also has the power to make him feel like a Taco Bell Chi-wawa.

The woman is so powerful, that her words can penetrate a man's heart- just as the actions of a man can move a woman's heart into a totally different direction.

Show me one woman who does not like a man who gets more things done then he talks about?

Gradually, you will find that the more you begin to accomplish in life through

God, the less you can talk about doing it. Because you have to reserve your energy for two things, getting it done, and praising God for helping you get it done. Good relationships are built upon sacrifice and anticipation.

Without you I might not be moving no where —

Without me , you might be moving in the wrong direction —

That's what y'all will be able to say.

Doors of Destiny

The doors to your destiny are motion activated.

Don't let satan push you into thinking the doors are locked, because God already went ahead and unlocked them all for you. If you don't have the faith to walk towards them, how will you have the faith to walk through them?

"Truly I tell you, if anyone says to this mountain, 'Go, throw yourself into the sea,' and does not doubt in their heart but believes that what they say will happen, it will be done for them. (Mark 11:23) Note and keep in mind that if you are woking with God, it will be done for you.

You won't have to move the mountain, you just have to have the faith that it will be moved.

Just as David was handed the victory with Goliath. If you pursue victory, you shall find it.

Knock and the door will be answered. God already has your victory waiting for you behind the next door, so keep on going until you receive it.

Vision to Move Forward

Just as satan can cause you to walk around in a circle—or backwards like you are blind.

God can cause you to be able to walk around without even needing to use your physical sight to get you to the destination before time runs out.

God can get you there ahead of time.

Time out.

How he do this?

Well if you believe in God , you have to start believing in the Holy Spirit you hear talking to you, and choose to make God the director of your life.

Then he will give you directions that no man even knew existed.

Believe Into Victory

1 Corinthians 10:11
"God won't give you more than you can handle"
And he always gives you a way out.
With God all things are possible.
If you feel broken with your back against the wall, then you need to tell satan to get off your territory and start expressing gratitude for the solutions God is going to

give you. Ask for your way out.

Sometimes for you to be given the directions on what to do, you have to stop grieving for false reality of failure which seems to plague your life.

If you need direction , then you must first pray

Matthew 6:6 "But when you pray, go into your room, close the door and pray to your Father, who is unseen. Then your Father, who sees what is done in secret, will reward you."

He will reveal what is unseen

As faith is the evidence of things unseen.

To move forward you're going to have to use your faith.

Hebrews 11:11 "And by faith even Sarah, who was past childbearing age, was enabled to bear children because she considered him faithful who had made the promise."

Pray for your eyes to be opened, and they shall be! "And Elisha prayed, 'Open his eyes, Lord, so that he may see." - II Kings 6:17

The book of Judges 4-7 also shows how the believer should not be afraid. It says not to worry because it is your enemies who are afraid, they live in fear and you live in victory.

This is why you are called believers, because you believe.
So start believing.

You are waiting on God and God is waiting on your Spirit.

The scripture says do not take cowards into battle with you.
This is true.
What also is true , is that sometimes your flesh is your only hold up to your breakthrough.
I believe it's called breakthrough because your perfect self which is loaded

into your spirit is waiting to break through your flesh,
Thus revealing your true purpose and potential. A loaded spirit means God put everything inside of you , you ever would need to be great.
You have to pull it out.
The flesh will adjust, but starts off weak,
however the spirit has strength to establish the impossible , through God on Earth.

As long as you keep your confidence in God and keep your flesh tamped down, you will be able to let your spirit rule over you,
God then can surely use you and prosper you.
The scripture in Judges, shows God will deliver what you need into your hand— so you shall not worry.
But it can only be delivered into your spiritual hand. Your spiritual hand can then

posses it on earth with your flesh.

The issue folks is not that God is not delivering you your blessings here on earth,

he is waiting to deliver them to you in your right spiritual state.

Ever heard the phrase "Gotta go and get it"
Well with God it's already been made available but you have to get it — your spirit has the power to

believe and then receive it for you here on earth, something your flesh cannot do by itself.

Your spirit has the access keys to God's Kingdom and you have to obediently believe to use them.

Your spirit is where the power is at.

If you can learn how to walk in the spirit, and not the flesh ,

You will know to do things other people don't.
You will be in perfect alignment with God , because through Jesus , you have been made the righteousness of God. "2 Corinthians 5:21Amplified Bible (AMP)
"He made Christ who knew no sin to [judicially] be sin on our behalf, so that in Him we would become the righteousness of God [that is, we would be made

acceptable to Him and placed in a right relationship with Him by His gracious lovingkindness]."

And if you walk in the divine , you will be in divine timing.

You see, God can trust your spiritual hands because those hands are the ones with the righteous discernment on how to manage what needs to be managed and bless seed to where seed needs to be sowed. But , you have to grow into that person, by revealing your true spirit. You have to honestly use your blessings, and fulfill your purpose on Earth. God wants you to be prosperous, but prosperous with purpose.

If you can make it rain at the strip club
you can make it rain at Kroger when old people can't afford their food.

Let the Holy Spirit guide you.

It's not about giving to the poor unchecked, it is about giving to the meant to receive person at that specific moment. God may tell you to pass one person and buy a house for the next.

We're all perfectly equipped to receive Gods blessings—the question is are we in the right position and frame of mind to hear it and do it.

Fail Safe One

God ins't denying you anything, you are denying yourself !
You can only access the vault of blessings by using your spirit man.
The scripture in Matthew 19:23 shows " its hard for a rich man to enter into the kingdom of heaven, it's easier for him to pass through the eye of a needle."

It's not that a rich man cannot enter in, but you have to gain access the right way. You gain access through using your spirit , not your prideful flesh. You don't need your riches, to accept God's riches. Because God's riches are unlimited. How do you walk in the spirit ? By rejecting your flesh, and maintaining your confidence in the word and promises of God.

Therefore you walk a different way, you problem solve a different way, you expect things and see life a different way.

God teaches you these ways by his word. For example, you can expect poverty if you see it, or you could understand that there is no lack in the word of God and in fact believe he has "blessed you with a surplus of prosperity" (Deuteronomy 28:11) eventually you will see this manifest in your life.

Opportunities are Bountiful

With God opportunities are numerous.
But believing in God is taking advantage of them.
Why didn't you take advantage of the opportunity?
Because you didn't think it would work?
Where did that false truth of self-doubt come from?
The enemy!

The person who believes in God would've said : "Be it on to me" and expect for it to work- that's faith.
The other was fear.
Speed up or slow down,
Your choice.
Some people say if you're focused
you won't take hold of all opportunities.
That's truer than true.
    Satan don't just steal the right opportunities , he

offers you the wrong ones to trip you up.

The truth is, a divinely focused mind is tuned to noticed the plot's of the adversary and angels are equipped to war against them , if you bring them into battle.

Bodybuilding with God

To be a true follower of God you must have the discipline of a Bodybuilder.

Why?

because

A bodybuilder operates around normal people and countless distractions whether it's through **useless works outs** or **undisciplined emotional eating**.
(Resisting the Devil)

Yet, they maintain their **personalized planned goals. (Operate in Victory)** They also know **exactly what goal (Clear Vision , Clear uncluttered thinking and decision making- no double mind)** what it is they are trying to achieve, they don't eyeball their portions or weight , they measure and compare it to their goal **(Live according to the Word)**, because they knew exactly what it was they

wanted to be and where they **wanted to go.** And the greatest bodybuilders **visualize**, not only the **end goal** but every **muscle contraction. (Follow it through uncompromisingly with righteousness)**

Provision with God

Some people secretly say why even plan?
"Not going to make it anyway."

Believing in God is having a plan.
Believing in God is then taking sudden action on the plan.
Believing in God is making sudden changes to the

"plan" when the Holy Spirit instructs.

Believing in God is making bold moves on the plan when the Holy Spirit delivers revelation.

Believing in God is doing the impossible.

Believing in God is believing there is a God and his power is real.

Believing in God is believing in a God who is alive in you, and also above you, but who has given you the power to continue the development of the Universe.

Believing in God is knowing he's given you the keys to drive the Maserati while others out here trying only to wash the car.
Believing in God is to be a bold, quick decision maker with no regrets.
Believing in God entitles you to unlimited victories and miracles. Just as the

widow is 2 Kings 4 was told to fill vessels with oil, she was told to gather as many as she could.

And the word says that when she ran out of vessels to place the oil, the oil stops. This means that if she had even greater amount of vessels the oil would still flow.

God's wear-house, known as Heaven is full of miracles designed for us to have. It is up to us to keep taking

advantage of them. It's unlimited !
Believing in God is changing your speech to align with the power of his word.
Believing in God is foreseeing the future.
Believing in God delivers uncommon common sense — known as Godly wisdom.
Believing in God is not caring what it looks like.
Believing in God is not being bamboozled by false

non-realities or vain deceit and idol fantasy.

Believing in God is living with a standard.

Believing in God is knowing what is right and wrong based off of each unique situation and guidance of the Holy Spirit. Believing in God is knowing your imperfection has always been your opportunity for perfection.

Believing in God is knowing there is no wall or fight, only

cultivation, only momentum riding, re-directing of energy (like Bruce Lee). Ultimately, you know everything is going to workout in your favor.

Believing in God is rejecting all negative memo's.
Believing in God is calling it like it is *suppose to be.*
Believing in God is taking vengeance.
Vengeance is taking pleasure in setting Sh*t straight, according to truth.

The scripture says in Proverbs 10:12 that "Hatred stirs up conflict , but love covers over all wrongs."
Well since love is anticipation, I anticipate you might not know right from wrong so Imma try and teach you.
If I hate you , I could not give a dam* and leave you ignorant.
But I love you, so I teach.
Proper vengeance is catching the conflict before

it happens and setting things straight. This includes proper education, real love, and forgiveness.

While believing in God, being timid is not an option; being bold as a lion is your only option. The Lord is my Shepard, I shall not want. He giveth his beloved sleep. God said whatever I put my hands to do shall prosper. I am prospering. My Body is the temple of the Holy Spirit. Holy Ghost, I am healed by the stripes of Jesus Christ. "If you believe it, Say it OUT LOUD and say AMEN!"

One thing at a time

The holy spirit will get you anything you ask.
It's like flying first class on Emirates.
Jesus said in Luke 11:9 "So I say to you: Ask and it will be given to you; seek and you will find; knock and the door will be opened to you. For everyone who asks receives; the one who seeks finds; and to the one who knocks, the door will be

opened....'Which of you fathers, if your son asks for a fish, will give him a snake instead? Or if he asks for an egg, will give him a scorpion? If you then, though you are evil, know how to give good gifts to your children, how much more will your Father in heaven give the Holy Spirit to those who ask him!"
The gift is of the Holy Spirit. The Holy Spirit is sent so that you can have Godly

wisdom , transcending man's wisdom;
gaining you anything you would ever need.
Even Jesus needed direction for perfecting his future.
So he turned to his Father and he sent him the Holy Spirit.
Jesus used the Holy Spirit and so shall you.
We must also remember to rejoice for the blessing of the Holy Spirit as Jesus did too.

The scripture says " In that same hour he (Jesus) rejoiced in the Holy Spirit and said, ' I thank you, Father, Lord of heaven and earth, that you have hidden these things from the wise and understanding…'
Blessed are the eyes which see what you see!"
Meaning you will see , even what the wise on earth cannot see.
If God sees the future.

He sends the Holy Spirit to you so you will too.
The spirit dwells with you to project for you, so that you can see what God sees — that being the future.
Give thanks for that.

What is Love 2

love, is the bold vengeance of setting stuff straight . because scripture says in 1 John 3:18
"Little children, let us love not in word and speech, but in action and truth. And by this we will know that we belong to the truth, and will assure our hearts in His presence: If our hearts condemn us, God is greater than our hearts, and He knows all things."

Love is anticipation then action.
1 john 3:5 says :
Jesus purpose was to set things straight.
"But you know that Christ appeared to take away sins, and in Him there is no sin."
satan from the beginning of the scripture tried to have things twisted.
He had people convinced they were sinners, and no good for God.

Rendering them paralyzed towards any meaningful faith filled action in overcoming the impossible.
Therefore Jesus' love was his passion for setting sh*&t straight.
Untwisting the truth.
The truth is, we are now able to be the righteousness of God , through
Christ Jesus,
we can enter into the Kingdom of God and accept our inheritances.

In a relationship the scenario would be, you know what, I see you aren't being treated right by the world, so I am going to stand up , MAN up and make you feel like a queen. I am going to help you set things straight by helping to remove your bondage.

Ephesians 5:25 confirms what I have just said. "Husbands, love your wives, just as Christ loved the church and gave himself up for her."

Righteous Success

When you have found yourself , you can walk freely from bondage.
That's the purpose of believing in God.
He is your reason and confirmation for cultivation.
The benefits of cultivation he leaves with you to discover.
That's called a blessing.

If you walk according to Jesus' journey and seek counsel with God,
you will be able to go fast, accurately, and toil free towards your successful life and destiny.
The weight and burden of sin , can no longer slow you down.
If you have faith in God, and know what he has meant for you is a blessing in store(age).

Then you can plan to pick it up and you will have whatsoever you ask when you pray believe and you shall have what you ask for (that is scripture).

You will have such abundance, unlimited protection, provisions, power, authority, and righteousness. Your blessing after you believe won't accept anything less.
You will be able to move mountains,

without barrier, if you believe
and be protected from all things.

In order to begin living in this lifestyle

God is simply waiting for you to believe and :

<u>See it (Vision)</u>

<u>Speak it (Faith)</u>

<u>Suddenly Act on it (Authority - Righteous Dominion)</u>

DO YOU BELIEVE?

YOUR BELIFE ACTIVATES YOUR BOLD REST of ACTION.

All he ask for in return is that you do things and use your power with his intention.

His intention is to see growth to all good things on Earth.

And to see you controlled by nothing but your own, heart, mind and soul.

Success is doing all that you knew you were capable of.

Accept his **power** and **authority** into your heart. **Believing** in God is **becoming** more.

If Only You Believe

If you believe in God.
God will be apart of the picture.
He will show up;
When it comes to riches
When it comes to dreams
When it comes to persistence
When it comes to bold confidence
When it comes to deliverance
When it comes to finances

When it comes to fiancé
When it comes to blessing others,
God shows up with you in your states of dominion, your states of love, and your states of creation.
If you can't include God in these areas,
you truly don't believe in God.
Believing in God is being available for him to operate effectively through you.

God's focus is on getting you to a perfected state. He wants to heal you, forgive you, and bless you tremendously.

Church will be where you run to when you are starving for the word.

But God goes beyond the church. God is in the most important place , and that is in you.

The truth is, many silence God.

He is silenced when people choose condemnation over grace.
He is silenced because "they" silence him.
Out of their condemnation they no longer feel righteous enough to accept God's blessing.
Pushing them into a state of non expectancy and disbelief. 1 John 5:14 says "And this is the confidence that we have toward him, that if we ask anything

according to his will he hears us."

You have to forge and maintain your confidence in God , by confidence in yourself.

You have to maintain the confidence that he hears.

If you feel like you are catching yourself in wrong things, then you loose confidence in yourself that God even would still have confidence in us. But through Christ Jesus, he has made us whole. So it is up to us, to step back into alignment with God.

"Beloved, if our hearts don't condemn us, we have boldness toward God;" (1 John 3:21)

You must maintain your boldness with God.

Your boldness is your confidence.

Just as the woman maintained boldness with Jesus in Matthew 15:23, she was able to accurately focus her laser attention on what she wanted from God, and through that sphere of bold confidence , received the blessing.

He is silenced by lack of belief.

He is silenced by the refusal to clean up your act, these are the hold up's of success with God.

God no longer remembers your wrongs when you repent.

But it is up to you to repent then to operate as a temple through which God can act, and communicate with.
Not being "Holy" but being one with your spirit. This is who you are truly meant to be.

Show Up So God Can Show Out

1. Jesus needs you not to be standing upon an unrighteous sea. Command that sea to be calm.
Sea of unrighteousness and doubt BE CALM NOW!
2. Don't back up, and don't be double minded. CONFUSION. STEP BACK FROM ME RIGHT NOW!

3. Stop going in circles.

DELAY REMOVE YOURSELF FROM MY REALM OF INFLUENCE , HOLD UP'S YOU ARE NO MORE!

4. Take pleasure in the word of God and resist the devil. (James 4:7)
WE SHALL HAVE DOMINION AND SUBDUE OVER THIS EARTH.. IT IS MINE. Just as Daniel was made ruler over all of Babylon , I shall be made to rule too.

5. Remove ARO (ANEXITY, RUSH, OPTIONS) CONFUSION, DEPRESSION YOU ARE NO LONGER VALID IN MY LIFE!

6. Remain in alignment to receive the revelation. SPIRIT OF STRENGTH AND BOLDNESS AND RIGHTEOUSNESS , DWELL WITH ME NOW AND FOREVER!

7: GPS (GODS PERSONAL SECRETARY) : GOD gives you his personal secretary (Holy Spirit) who will help re-route you until you get to your destination.
GOD, CONTINUE TO DIRECT ME IN THE PATH I AM TO GO.

8: Don't let the storm happening around you keep you from walking on water.
STORM BE QUIET!

9: Do things with Godly Intention.

GOD I SEEK TO DO THINGS WITH YOUR WILL! AMEN.

These are some steps you can take to show up so that God can show out.

What Happens when You Connect with God

When you believe in God you no longer have to wait on a deadline you just have to maintain your faith. When you believe in God, you don't want to see one thing move forward, you want to see all things move forward.
You no longer have to strive to be righteous.

You more naturally end up in a better state, and your tastes become more appropriate in accepting your righteousness .

You have a keen eye for deception and out-of-place things.

Your awareness becomes heightened.

Your sway becomes more bold.

You cringe from pride but accelerate into action.

You're passionate over seemingly un-meaningful things.

You become more caring and loving, making you genuine.

You're no longer a creation who's stagnate.

You become a creation in action communicating with the creator to create more. If you believe in God , you no longer have to toil.

Affliction

Thank you God for delivering me from (Affliction) a state of pain, distress, grief, and misery. And delivering me into a state of revelation, creation, prosperity, health, happiness, generosity, wisdom and mastery.
The person free from affliction is the person consumed with Godly direction.

God offers you the road of pleasure everyday. The pleasure of doing good things which lead you to victory and happiness.
Don't let satan convince you he is the only one who can give pleasure.
God is capable of turning your weaknesses into strengths and your mistakes into glory.
Sure you may be on a diet, but if a slice of pizza will cause you to have a

global praise report, EAT DAT SLICE OF PIZZA! AMEN , AMEN.

You just don't know, if the Holy Spirit placed it on your heart to eat that slice of pizza, it was because, God knew that when you went for a napkin you would come across a journal listing out the exact diet you must follow to reach your goal. Setting you free from that plateau, and carrying you higher. Not only were you giving praise while eating that slice of pizza , you now will continue to give God praise for your newly discovered resource. Don't be fooled, for the scripture in 1 Timothy 4: tells us to use our discerning spirit in determining the good God has created for us to enjoy. If you keep God apart of it, he is good to clean away all evil. "But the [Holy] Spirit

explicitly *and* unmistakably

declares that in later times some will turn away from the faith, paying attention instead to deceitful *and* seductive spirits and doctrines of
demons, [misled] by the hypocrisy of liars whose consciences are seared as with a branding iron [leaving them incapable of ethical functioning], who forbid marriage
and *advocate* abstaining from [certain kinds of] foods

which God has created to be gratefully shared by those who believe and have [a clear] knowledge of the truth. For everything God has created is <u>good</u>, (including sex with your wife and food) and nothing is to be rejected if it is received with gratitude; for it is sanctified [set apart, dedicated to God] by means of the word of God and prayer."

If you allow God to move you out of a state of affliction, setbacks, and misery , you will make room for him to move you into a state of ongoing prosperity. Do things by his will, and he will not forget yours. Psalms 34:19 scripture says " Many are the afflictions of the righteous , but the Lord will delivereth him out of them all. " If you schedule good things for your day.

God will schedule you out of the bad.

Learn to Speak the Language

Talking is the entertaining of uncertain faith. Have you noticed when you are trying to explain something or talk about something, you are analyzing it, trying to move it around until it makes sense?

However, you should speak over talking. Speaking is being able to go until you have enough power to command for your mountains to be moved. Once you reverberate sound from your heart, then the mountains begin to move. Heart producing sound is certainty, and certainty certainly moves mountains. The scripture says " Truly I tell you , if anyone says to this mountain , 'Go throw yourself into the sea and does not doubt in **their heart**….it will be done for them."

Those who talk do not act.
Those who speak, move mountains.
Therefore, you must learn how not to doubt and talk but to speak and act.
And when it comes to talking, there is no need to talk about it.
You are either believing it and working towards it, or standing upon your bold dominion and commanding it so.

Command until your heart believes, and you will begin to release your faith to do things for you. The scripture said "it will be done for them" not they will be able to do it.

Never be afraid of moving mountains, because when the right time comes , you won't have to.

Let Go

Have you ever seen a monkey?
It's like you can almost speak to it.
Part human, part not.
That's like your destiny if you let satan get involved in your belief.
You will be able to see your future,
but it will seem part reachable, yet so far away.

You must, with everything you got.
Seek God on his truth , resist the devil, and HE MUST FLEE.
When he flee's
Your future will become everything it was meant to be.Until you are laser focused , the breakthrough does not know who to go to.
Take for example in the scripture when Jesus was busy healing the people.

The lady who met rejection from Jesus but persisted, is a clear example of the ability to be relentless when you know what it is you are fighting for.

How many would of given up, if Jesus said no!

The scripture says Matthew 15:23 : "Jesus ignored her. The disciples came and complained, 'Now she's bothering us. Would you please take care of her? She's driving us crazy.' Jesus refused, telling them, "I've got my hands full dealing with the lost sheep of Israel." Then the woman came back to Jesus, went to her knees, and begged. "Master, help me." He said, "It's not right to take bread out of children's mouths and throw it to dogs." She was quick: "You're right, Master, but beggar dogs do get scraps from the master's table." Jesus gave in. "Oh, woman, your faith is something else. What you want is what you get!" Right then her daughter became well.

If you want to get breakthrough, you are going to have to breakthrough the cloud in your mind.

Once you establish clarity and come to terms with what it is you want!

Be bold in praying for what you want.

But just as you are bold , be clear too.

If you truly pray for your hearts desire, you shall see it come to past.

The reason why praying for money can be difficult is because satan can use that as a distraction point because he knows you don't really know what you want. And he can help confuse you , making it a reality that you don't know which direction the money is going to come in therefore you

start here, stop there, you circulate your
options and never really fully commit to anything.
Because you know the power of God is real, and the money is on the way but your prayers are vague, your focus is vague, you are not pointing your laser in any one specific direction therefore you are burning it out.
Think of this, ask for what you want, but become clear

with what it is you want and why.

It is ok to be specific with God,

your specifics will help lead you to satisfaction. If God has something better for you, ask for it.

Be clear for what you ask but also be open to receiving a greater blessing God may have in store for you.

Matthew 7:7

"Ask and it will be given to you; seek and you will find; knock and the door will be opened to you."

James 4:3

"And when you do ask, you do not receive, because you ask with wrong motives, that you may squander it on your pleasures."

1 John 5:14

"And this is the confidence that we have
before Him: If we

ask anything according to His will, He hears us. And if we know that He hears us in whatever we ask, we know that we already possess what we have asked of Him. ..."

Laser focus
ask for what you want
pray for what you want.

Hear the Heart

Don't go off feeling
go off Sound.
You are better equipped to match that reality.
Sound goes directly to the heart.
Feelings get caught up in the flesh.
"The voice is Jacob's voice, but the hands are the hands of Esau." And he did not recognize him, because his hands were hairy like his brother Esau's hands. So he

blessed him. (Genesis 27:22)

Issac made the mistake of choosing feeling over sound. Sometimes you are better able to hear what's right then use, your flesh to feel whats right. Because the sound is that which can go directly to your heart.

Make Weird Noises

How do I know if it's my calling or not?

When you can make weird noises while doing it
its your calling.
well why is that?
Because that is a human sign that you are no longer having to think about it.
You are dominating with no mind.

If you aren't using your mind, then you are 1o0% in the moment and in the spirit and your utterances do not make sense to man, but it does
make sense to God.
Your weird utterances is a joyful heart, shouting truth back to God.
Speak the blessing until you can hear it echo back to you from your heart.
When you can hear the echo from your heart match what

you said, then you know you are using Godly power.

Hearing Your Calling

Other people might can't hear your calling.
But you can.
Like the call of Samuel , it comes consistently .
If you were once excited about it , it is your calling --- if you lack excitement now that's because Satan has been at work , it requires meekness , steadfastness and prayer.

Stop thinking you wasted time.

Condemnation —— this is where things can get held up.
This is where my quote is very important " the only way you can be late is if you sit at Satan's stop light for too long."
Wisdom is knowing how to move around what's being held up and produce victory.

Blind Man with Three Blind Dice.

When you throw your dice, you want to win.

What if you had the choice to be in a state that when you threw your dice, you knew the outcome?

This is the type of power you have if you believe in God.

It's important we visit the story of Gideon,
Yet Again to illustrate it.

" The people of Israel went back to doing evil in the sight of God"....God put them under the domination of Midian for seven years....They left nothing for them to live on,....
See if we rewind it, we can remember that God always gives you enough to become debt free and enough to live off of. Once you step into the land of being blind to God.
You turn yourself off to this.

If you are gonna walk with other people's Gods you are basically giving away your gift and letting it spoil.
God sent them a prophet with this message: "God, the God of Israel, says,
I delivered you from Egypt,
   I freed you from a life of slavery;
I rescued you from Egypt's brutality
   and then from every oppressor;

I pushed them out of your way
    and gave you their land.
"And I said to you, 'I am God, your God. Don't for a minute be afraid of the gods of the Amorites in whose land you are living.' But you didn't listen to me."

Use Gideon's story to help you get right with reality. The reality is , God is faithful to bless all Godly things upon to you but you have to be faithful to receive.

Being faithful to receive means you do not willingly sin in the sight of the Lord. Not because God himself is judging you , but because you , yourself won't feel capable of receiving God's blessing.

You are the reason for the constant circles in your life. You are the starting and ending point to sabotage that happens in your life.

Not satan
Not God.
The Angel said to Gideon ….. " God is with you , O mighty warrior"…..
Gideon replied, "With *me*, my master? If God is with us, why has all this happened to us? Where are all the miracle-wonders our parents and grandparents told us about?"

The youth of today ask the same question in these streets.
If God is so good , where is he at?
God is waiting to make an appearance through you. That is where he is at.

Stop letting Satan use you to fight his own battles, become a Jerub-Baal (Let Baal fight his own battles.)
———-a person who removes

the hooks of the adversary out of their life.

If you roll with God, then sometimes you have to roll alone.

Sometimes, you have to pull up to the race in a broke down car.

Sometimes you have to become sick, so that you know why you will become well.

Sometimes you have to be a sinner so you know why you want to become a winner.

Sometimes the odds have to look so against you , that when you win , you can only give praise to God.

God said to Gideon, "You have too large an army with you. I can't turn Midian over to them like this—they'll take all the credit, saying, 'I did it all myself,' and forget about me. Make a public announcement: 'Anyone afraid, anyone who has any qualms at all, may leave Mount Gilead now and go home.'" Twenty-two companies headed for home. Ten companies were left.

God said to Gideon: "There are still too many. Take them down to the stream and I'll make a final cut. When I say, 'This one goes with you,' he'll go. When I say, 'This one doesn't go,' he won't go." So Gideon took the troops down to the stream." It's not that God didn't want Gideon to win, he just was waiting to make a move when the odds seemed impossible to man, so that when victory came, there was no one else to be given the glory for it, but GOD! Sometimes the only thing that is holding you back is your lack of giving God praise. Think about it.

The victory has already been won.

So start rejoicing!

Samson's Death

Samson's death could be used to show that even in your death satan can still be defeated.

Then Samson prayed to the Lord, "Sovereign Lord, remember me. Please, God, strengthen me just once more, and let me with one blow get revenge on the Philistines for my two eyes.' Then Samson reached toward the two central pillars on which the temple stood. Bracing himself against them, his right hand on the one and his left hand on the other, Samson said, 'Let me die with the Philistines!' Then he pushed with all his might, and down came the temple on the rulers and all the people in it. Thus he killed many more when he died than while he lived." - Judges 16:28

Our comeback can be greater than ever before , if

you sincerely ask God for help.

Also make sure not to leave your blessings with the wrong people.

Stop dwelling in the wrong places , just because they please you. Samson's road to his partial defeat began with being with the wrong women. One after another he dated foreign women from foreign land. Not women who was of his heritage or cloth. This is important to note today. Having a woman who understands your family stature and Godly purpose is key. A woman who does not cunningly seek for your defeat but wishes greatness for your family.

" But his father and mother said to him.. ' Is there not a woman among the daughters of your kinsmen, or among all your people, that you must go to take a wife from …. BUT…….

"she pleased Samson very well."

Well , don't let that be the reason for being in the wrong place with the wrong woman. Satan, will use moments of pleasure to turn into future moments of torment , if you let him. Gradually, over time, you have to beware of how the adversary sends what you like to get you to be where you are not suppose to be.

The enemy starts you off with a little bit lie, a little bit temptation.

Just as we see in the scriptures that led to Samson's death, his first wife was told to entice Samson so that he would be swindled. They told her to give them the answer to his riddle, so that they would win the wealth he had put up.

She enticed him alright, and got the answer and gave it to them.

But if you pay close attention, the answer to the riddle was something she should of known, as he did. Because they both were at the same place where the answer to the riddle was made , as seen in Judges 14:7-8. But she always meant to be a distraction for him, that is why she never even noticed what was

important to him— Satan wanted to use her to destroy him. But God turned it into a learning lesson for Samson, yet it was up to him to recognize it, and turn from his wicked ways.
This should of been a red flag to Samson to watch out, for he knows now, this is how the enemy is rolling against him.
Using a woman to entice him and pleasure him for

gain that in turn would lead to his destruction.

Remember your great strength lies within you, but comes out of you through help of the Holy Spirit, just as Samson made great victories, this happened when the spirit came over him.

Satan's game is to get you into a place where he can hold you back from being in connection with the Holy Spirit, in the hopes he can hold you back from your victories.

This is perhaps one of the biggest lessons. It, is to stop allowing the enemy to stop you from living a righteous life of doing boldly God's work.

What you are suppose to do , if you believe in God , is enter into seemingly impossible situations and come out having dominated and defeated them. Then it is your place to give praise

to God for what he has done.
This is the process.
Preparation and all those other philosophies only work in certain situations.
But this is the key to life.
Be alive , and receptive in the Holy Spirit and word of God and with God you shall achieve all things.

Under the Law

When you are under the law, you are punished for disobeying it, and you are responsible for it.
However, Jesus came and took away that responsibility.
An example can be found in the scripture of 2 Samuel 24, when David was troubled with the Lord.
It explains how he was approached by a servant of

God and asked which punishment he wanted to choose.

" Shall three years of famine come to you…. or will you flee and be pursued…or shall there be three days of pestilence in your land?" David said all his righteousness was by his hand, but now our righteousness was achieved by Jesus' hand and we just have to accept it. No longer must we worry about the lord rewarding us according to our righteousness [2 Samuel 22:21] now we are able to say "Praise be to the God and Father of our Lord Jesus Christ! In his great mercy he has given us new birth into a living hope through the resurrection of Jesus Christ from the dead," as found in 1 Peter 1:3. " God made him who had no sin to be sin for us, so that in him we might become the righteousness of God." (2 Corinthians 5:21)

Enough said.

Go and live free.

Man's Discipline

A Man who believes in God, is a man who does not allow the enemy to defeat him.
As the scripture says, we were not created for wrath but instead for glory.
A Man brings light.
A Man is suppose to save the day.
A Man is suppose to be counted on and come through.

A Man has no room for excuses because they wouldn't look good next to his results.

A Man sees what needs to be done ahead of time and get its done.

A Man is strong and resists temptation.

A Man realizes that his power rest with God.

A Man is sharper than a sword but lets the noble woman shine.

A Man makes miracles for other people.

Turning Unclean to Clean

Go and possess that unclean land.

It doesn't matter if the land is unclean

Go

Clean it and possess it.

Out of the cement cracks in the ghetto, a flower can grow.

Ezra 9:11

"Now, our God, what shall we say after this? For we have forsaken Your commandments, which You

have commanded by Your servants the prophets, saying, 'The land which you are entering to possess is an unclean land with the uncleanness of the peoples of the lands, with their abominations which have filled it from end to end and with their impurity."
God is saying that you have the authority to clean, unclean land.

The purpose is to take dominion and subdue the land. No serpent of twisted energy can stand on your territory unless you allow it. Through Christ Jesus, you have been made righteous to take back full righteous dominion.

Adam had the authority but he did not subdue the serpent. He allowed the threat to roam free.

He had the authority to cast the serpent off his territory but did not.

This allowed Eve to encounter a force which should of been defeated by man, before it had the opportunity to operate it's agenda.

It may seem hard, but resisting the devil and casting him out is the first step towards taking authority back over your land.

To know God

Thanks to Jesus, we all are able to have a direct connection with God.
Jesus has cleansed us from anything that would stand between our connection with God.
It simply requires you believe in what he has done, and what is there to be taken by you.

You must accept Christ and allow that belief to come into your heart.

In French Savoir means " to know"

If someone saves you , they don't have to know you, but you bet your bottom dollar, you're gonna want to know them. Well Jesus, saved us. So get to know him.

Don't Accept It

Alright so we've all come to the conclusion that God has been waiting on us.
But the funny thing is, all the condemnation of you being less-than, a failure, or a late individual to everything— especially the important matters of life, is in fact a lie from Satan.

Don't accept it.

Turn your thought pattern around right now by saying OUT LOUD :

I am the righteousness of God

I have and always will be on time, in the right place at the right time.

God has protected me from being spoiled for my glory to come.

He has already made available my prosperous, divine destiny.

I shall use my blessings from God to establish the Kingdom of God here on earth.
I am successful ,
I am prominent
I am resourceful
I will continue to have breakthroughs
I will fulfill my destiny
No one else will be allowed to do that which I am meant to do.
I am transforming

I have transformed into the powerful spirit I am meant to be.

I am perfectly who I need to be for this moment.

True Sin

I heard a preacher say that
Adam was the first to sin in
the Garden of Eden,
Not Eve,
Because when God created
man,
he created him and gave
him dominion and told him
to subdue all things.
Therefore, he had the
righteous authority from
God to subdue the serpent

with it's twisted lies and cast him out
thus doing what a man should do— protecting his family from evil.
If he had done this, his wife, Eve would not of had an encounter.
Even more, Adam would of been able to boldly decree that they would do nothing but listen to God
and rule over their kingdom and territory.

Just as it is read in the Book of Ezra " For we have forsaken your commandments, which you commanded by your servants the prophets, saying , "The land which you are entering, to take possession of it" (Ezra 9:10) It later goes on to reveal that the land which you are must enter and subdue may seem to be unclean , but God has mandated you to clean it up.

Set sh*^t straight.
It's like being the equalizer.
Therefore, the true sin is not in making the mistake,
the hold up is in not getting to the root of the problem and cleaning it out.
If you believe in God , then you should know, that through Christ Jesus you were made righteous to take dominion over your home, future home, life and territory.

Understand, evil is no longer a force that can prevail against you.

Straighten up and set things in your life right.

Just as Confucius describes the process of becoming more appropriate and it's positive effects on the entire family, this rings true in the Bible.

If the leader is all messed up , the clan will suffer too.

Therefore, you must take back your authority and walk

in it, and nothing can come against you in Jesus name.

Heart Reviving

Understand God grants you reviving through your bondage but needs you to gain hold of something deeper — listening to the discerning Godly spirit in your heart. This happens by belief in God.

Ezra 9:8 explains this level of clarity with saying " And now for a little moment grace hath been shed from Jehovah our God, to leave us a remnant to escape, and to give us a nail in his holy place, that our God may lighten our eyes, and give us a little reviving in our bondage."

The freedom from bondage comes from excepting the freedom from God.

Heart Reader

Ever known the answer by just looking at a person, or feeling what you heard instead of actually hearing what you heard? This is the benefit of being able to have a spirit within you that can communicate and direct with your heart to come to understandings that , the evil doers would choose you not to have.

Revelation is both a tool from God to reveal greater

visions for your life, and a tool for you to protect the one you have. In order though to fully process , with your heart. You must,

1. Understand the power in your heart.
2. Be able to read other people heart's : 1 Samuel 16:7 "…for the lord sees not as man sees; man looks on the outward appearance, but the Lord looks on the heart."

Although your flesh will see the what it looks like on the outside, you must seek for God to inspire your spirit to see what's going on behind the scenes, this is discernment.
3. Creating with heart. : David accepted the challenge and spoke victory.

Victory starts in the heart, then translates out into the world.

Cravings

Many think that if you believe in God, you have to subdue your cravings and ignore them. This thinking is twisted— wholesome cravings are designed to help you crave what you are missing in your life. Therefore, in the process of accepting your righteousness of God made available to you through Christ Jesus. You'll will naturally begin to crave the new more appropriate choices. This requires your willingness to accept God's way, and Jesus' lifestyle while subduing directly what's been holding you back in life.

1 Timothy 4:4 reads "For everything God has created is good, and nothing is to be rejected if it is received with gratitude; for it is sanctified [set apart, dedicated to God] by means

of the word of God and prayer."

Learn to pray to God if you are in question. Because if you pray, God is quick in this manner to answer and reveal.

Before Jesus

Before Jesus , the Spirit of the Lord had to come down upon people by God's choosing.

After Jesus , the Spirit of the Lord walks with you and helps you, upon you choosing to believe in him. When you choose him, you should begin giving praise to God for giving you blessings in all your endeavors ; "to have success in all my undertakings." 1 Samuel 18:14.

Click Over

Ask God to re-activate you. Just as found in Ezra , even in captivity , they prayed and acknowledge the power of God to activate, set in motion, and renew them. If you feel down and out. You must be the one to get up , jump and shout, and believe that you will regain your boldness by walking the rest of your path in alignment with God.

Financial Savings

God wants you to have a savings.

A store house, and extra money to live off of and be a blessing with.

Having a savings. This is crucial in being able to reject the influence of satan. So if you don't have a powerful savings, cast Satan off of your financial property. Remember Issac got richer and richer by the day. This was by Gods release. Promote yourself to allow God to release new blessings upon you.

Three things I learned in India

Residue - the evil spirit tries to cling on you, but wash yourself in the Holy Spirit and the word of God and it will come off you, the demonic stupors have to leave because of Jesus Christ blood already shed which took it away. You have to believe this happened. And for the record it is historical. It did happen.

In India, they teach that people walk around with residue, ever approach a stranger and feel repelled by them? That is because they are possessing an invisible residue, that is visible to the spiritual eye.

Dharma - simple…. doing that which you know you should be doing at that very moment.

Replacing old bad habits, with new more appropriate habits- is this not the pathway God has given us to greatness? This is also the true definition of Yoga.

What I learned from studying Confucius

Is that the whole family, the whole village the whole world, suffers when you fail to become more. When you fail to refine yourself, you fail to deliver blessings to the world.

It is your noble responsibility to live will discipline, honor, and decree.

Walk upright young man , Walk upright.

What I learned in Chinese Martial Arts

The mind moves, the spirit stands still. Meditation trains your focus not to move so much.

The world believes that if you focus on one thing you win.

Truth is, if you focus with one thing —- that being faith, then always you will win. Don't get it twisted. God is not limited, he is unlimited.

Fear, apprehension, caution are all signs of trying to accomplish things on your own.

However unique boldness, true character, bold redemption and silent discipline are all signs of walking with God.

Thinking if you invest your all into that one thing is not the same as giving all of your faith to one thing.

You have to keep your mind where God is.

Holiness with Meaning

Have you ever heard the saying: "He the MAN!"

"The Man" just means he who operated like Jesus. This is what the scripture means as holiness.

Well just as Dr. Creflo Dollar said, holiness is not an action it is a man. It was Jesus. It is he who is holiness, is the man. Until you can switch over to "The perfected state, you can't penetrate victory. It's like in Lord of the Rings, Gandalf had the sauce, he had the fabric to cast demons out, but until he went all bright light — commanding bold victory did he move mountains and shift the status of the war. (First he had to die, thus death to the weak flesh).

He needed to go to "Da Man" status, which is life to the spirit man.

Anyone who does great things goes into " Da Man" status.

This is the victory God has left to all of us.

So we all have the ability to be the "Man" that is considered holy. It is being one with Jesus, it is the same for everyone. Like Neo, you can become the one.

A Noble Life

It would take too long to read all the ways on how to live a noble disciplined life. So Jesus loved us so much he prayed and he fasted, he sacrificed so that we would get a shot once again at being like God.

To have the Holy Ghost be apart of your life is the most majestic thing possible.

This spirit, is the one which will walk with you, and show you God is real.

Once you can see God is real. You my friends will truly be able to believe.